NONE
DARE
CALL
IT
TREASON!

BOOK 17

The Supreme Court
A   Devastating Threat
To
National Security!

Robert W. Pelton
$4.95

*"Treason doth
never prosper,*

"What's the reason?

"Why if it prosper,

"None dare call it

treason."

John Harrington

Printed in America
On Recycled Paper
In
Charleston, South Carolina

Published in America
By
The Freedom & Liberty
Foundation Press
Knoxville, Tennessee

Dedicated
To
My Beloved
America

The greatest, most generous, most benevolent and most powerful nation on the face of the earth – and the only country in the history of the world to have been founded on Biblical principles.

A nation can survive its fools, and even the ambitious.

But it cannot survive treason from within.

An enemy at the gates is less formidable, for he is known and he carries his banners openly.

The traitor moves among those within the gates freely, his sly whispers rustling through the galleys, heard in the very hall of government itself.

For the traitor appears not traitor. He speaks in the accent familiar to his victims, and he wears their face and their garments, and he appeals to the baseness that lies deep in the hearts of all men.

He rots the soul of a nation - he works secretly and unknown in the night to undermine the pillars of a city - he infects the body politic so that it can no longer resist.

A murderer is less to be feared.

Cicero, 42 B.C.

CONTENTS

Forward

Independence Hall Where the Declaration of Independence Was Signed.

Our glorious Declaration of Independence is a timeless divinely inspired masterpiece given to mankind through the anointed pen of Thomas Jefferson.

The grand and unmatched United States Constitution is indisputably the product of Providential guidance and wisdom and certainly not a document which evokes whimsical interpretations with the changing political climates.

All Americans have a moral obligation to stand up and be counted in these trying times!

Abraham Lincoln boldly declared: *"To sin by silence when they should protest, makes cowards of men."*

William Lloyd Garrison capsulized it best: *"As a free man who is determined to remain free -- I do not wish to think or speak, or write with moderation.*

"Tell a man whose house is on fire to give a moderate alarm; tell him to moderately rescue his wife from the hands of a ravisher; tell the mother to gradually extricate her babe from the fire into which it has fallen -- but urge me not to use moderation in a course like the present."

Senator Barry Goldwater, 1964 Presidential candidate was castigated and verbally crucified by the media.

14

He simply stated this simple truism: *"Extremism in the pursuit of Liberty is no vice."*

This good and moral man of character soundly rocked the boat of the propagandists. He was as a result soundly defeated in the election.

The alarmed media wolves panicked the voters with their jeers and sneers and insane howls about this man's lack of *"moderation!"*

It can honestly be said that through the Providential genius of our Founding Fathers, the remaining remnants of the original American *Constitutional Republic* still provides more freedom, opportunity and abundance for mankind than is found in any other nation in the world.

This is true despite decade after decade of unabated treason and treachery promulgated by innumerable traitorous individuals found buried in the twiddle dee – twiddle dum administrations of both the Democrats and the Republicans.

 An informed and active, not a media brainwashed electorate, is the only antidote to further prostitution of, and the ultimate destruction of, what Benjamin Franklin called our Republic.

Preface

"Treason against the United States shall consist only in levying war against them, or in adhering to their enemies, giving them aid and comfort."

U.S. Constitution. Article 111, Section 3

What is your treason I.Q.?

If you can answer the following questions, it's high.

If you miss one or more, you should read the *None Dare Call It Treason* series!

Who was behind allowing Red Chinese soldiers take airborne training at Fort Benning, Georgia?

Is this not treason?

Why was South Vietnam, South Africa, Rhodesia and numerous other American friends deliberately betrayed to the forces of evil?

Is this not treason?

Why was our friend Chiang Kai Shek not so gently coerced into a Communist dictatorship by highly placed subversives in the State Department?

Is this not treason?

Why was Cuba treasonously delivered into the clutches of Communist revolutionary Fidel Castro?

Is this not treason?

Why have untold millions of dollars consistently been used to prop up faltering Red dictatorships and to assist Communist terrorists in overthrowing non-Communist governments?

Is this not treason?

What American company sold nuclear reactors to Communist Occupied Romania?

Is this not treason?

Name the company that provided Communist Hungary with a factory designed to make 1.5 million light bulbs daily?

Is this not treason?

What well known oil company invested $1 billion for oil exploration in Communist Occupied Angola?

Is this not treason?

Can you name the American company who treasonously built and equipped a $10 million electronics plant near Warsaw for the Polish slave labor tyranny?

Is this not treason?

These are questions to which every American should rightfully have an honest answer.

Unfortunately most do not!

Tragedy was carefully orchestrated by traitors in our Government and the media with regard to Cuba, Vietnam, Laos, Cambodia, Rhodesia, China, El Salvador, Nicaragua and many other countries. Anastasio Somoza was the former President of free Nicaragua.

He offered this startling insight in his 1980 book, Nicaragua Betrayed: *"I have factual evidence that the betrayal of Nicaragua was not perpetrated out of ignorance, but rather by design."*

Somoza was soon after assassinated!

Is this not treason?

John Lehman, Secretary of the Navy, made this shocking statement on May 25 to the 1983 Annapolis graduating class: *"Within weeks many of you will be looking across just hundreds of feet of water at some of the most modern technology ever invented in America.*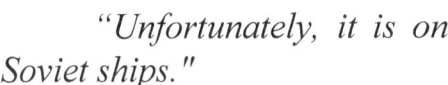

"Unfortunately, it is on Soviet ships."

Is this not treason?

Earl E.T. Smith was the American Ambassador to

Cuba when it was similarly delivered to the Communists.

He makes this concise comment on July 14, 1986: *"Nicaragua is Cuba all over again."*

Can you name the company that paid the Communist dictatorship in Angola over $600 million annually in taxes and oil royalties.

This money bought new Soviet jets, tanks and helicopter gunships.

And it paid Castro for supplying 35,000 imported Cuban mercenaries who keep the Angolan people enslaved.

Is this not treason?

Stressed retired Brigadier General Andrew J. Gatsis on August 11, 1986: *"Though aware of the Communist goal of world domination, the average U.S. Citizen refuses to believe that the real threat comes from governmental officials and their non-governmental confederates who secretly espouse the same objectives as the openly avowed Communists."*

Anthony Sutton stated in his 1986 book *The Best Enemy Money Can Buy:* "We now have the *formidable task of bringing these gentlemen to the bar of justice to publicly answer for their private and concealed actions."*

The *None Dare Call It Treason* series certainly won't win accolades from the United Nations or the State Department!

Nor will Harvard feel compelled to bestow an honorary degree upon the author!

Harvard Law School was the spawning ground for an incredible number of Red agents. Included were members of the first Soviet spy ring ever to be exposed in our government.

Reed Irvine aptly commented in July of 1986: *"Indeed, it has long been a joke among refugees from Eastern Europe that there are more Marxists at Harvard than there are in the Soviet Union, or Poland, or whatever Communist country the refugee called home."*

23

The Honorable Ezra Taft Benson said:

"The truth must be told even at the risk of destroying, in large measure, the influence of men who are widely respected and loved by the American people.

"The stakes are high. Freedom and survival is the issue."

Treason is still a most serious federal offense.

The *None Dare Call It Treason* series examines the reasons for and the Americans behind the fall of freedom and the rise of tyranny throughout the world!

Has anything really changed?
You Decide!

Treason

Whoever, owing allegiance to the United States, levies war against them or adheres to their enemies, giving them aid and comfort within the United States or elsewhere, is guilty of treason and shall suffer death, or be imprisoned not less than five years and fined not less than $10,000; and shall be incapable of holding any office under the United states.

U.S. Code, Title 18, Section 2381

Whoever, owing allegiance to the United States and having knowledge of the commission of any treason against them, conceals and does not, as soon as may be, disclose and make known the same to the President or to some judge of the United States, or to the Governor or to some judge or justice of a particular state, is guilty of misprision of treason, and shall be fined not more than $1000 or imprisoned not more than 7 years or both.   *U.S. Code, Title 18, Section 2382*

The Supreme Court

A Devastating Threat

To

National Security!

Treason: *"duplicity . . . breach of trust . . . disloyalty, treacherousness."*
The Merriam-Webster Thesaurus

Security risk Dean Acheson started out in government as Roosevelt's Under Secretary of the Treasury in 1933.

He'd been vigorously recommended by and was the protége of Felix Frankfurter of Harvard who would later be appointed an Associate Justice of the Supreme Court in 1939.

Felix Frankfurter was known at the time to be a Communist agent.

Despite this, he was appointed by FDR to the Supreme Court!

This subversive was a radical attorney who once filed charges against the Justice Department because of its anti-Communist activities.

Frankfurter became one of the *"Insiders"* in President Woodrow Wilson's *"Braintrust"* In 1917.

Former President Theodore Roosevelt stated unequivocally that Frankfurter's attitude was *"fundamentally that of Trotsky and the other Bolshevik leaders in Russia."*

Frankfurter joined with notorious leftist Roger Baldwin.

They founded the despicable anti-American ACLU on January 12, 1920!

The American Civil Liberties Union is a nonprofit organization.

It started as a nonpartisan roomful of civil rights activists and grew to an organization with more than 500,000 members and supporters.

Closely collaborating with Frankfurter and Baldwin were none other than identified Communists Elizabeth Gurley Flynn and William Z. Foster.

The organization can be found in the major cities of most states.

It handles an annual case load of close to 6,000 court cases.

Unfortunately a great many of the most prominent court cases over the years have been in support of politically left causes.

And in defense of known Communists and Communist causes.

Felix Frankfurter was a shadowy and carefully protected and promoted Red mole as were so many of his contemporaries.

A carefully orchestrated pattern of cover up of other moles by other moles planted throughout government and the press continued right on up to notorious Henry Kissinger and innumerable others subversives in between.

He was the patron of leftist Democrat William J. Brennan, Jr.

Brennan was not surprisingly President Eisenhower's choice for a seat on the Supreme Court!

Frankfurter recommended his protégés for government service while he taught at Harvard.

These included communists spies Harry Dexter White, Alger Hiss, Harold Glasser, and Lee Pressman!

All were scholastically bright but intellectually stunted Harvard clones who became Kremlin espionage agents!

Communist espionage agent Lee Pressman along with Dean Acheson had been one of Stalin's attorneys in the United States long before Communist Occupied Russia gained recognition from Washington!

Soviet agent Alger Hiss, Acheson's protégé, was indicted for perjury on December 15, 1949.

He'd lied to a Federal Grand Jury when questioned about his spying service to Moscow as a Communist mole!

Hiss should rightfully have been indicted for treason!

He was instead found guilty on January 21, 1950, by Judge Henry W. Goddard, on two counts of perjury and given a five year sentence.

This espionage agent was then released on $10,000 bail, pending an appeal.

Elevated to Secretary of State under Truman, Acheson stood firmly behind his intimate friend.

He declared on January 25, 1950, that *"whatever the outcome"* of the appeal, *I do not intend to turn my back on Alger Hiss!"*

Senator Joseph R. McCarthy commented: *"What clearer signal could have been given to the traitors and potential traitors in government?*

*"They were assured of support from the highest offici*als in our government."

Hiss served less than four years in prison.

As could be expected, he became a martyr and a folk hero to the Communists and the so-called liberal-left element in the United States.

The mystery still remains unanswered as to why Alger Hiss wasn't tried under the existing espionage laws, or better yet, tried for treason!

Less than four years in a federal penitentiary is a relatively light sentence for a traitor!

Michael Straight was a fellow Red who once criticized Acheson for publicly supporting Hiss!

This Communist conspirator charged Acheson with *"indulging in a personal luxury that could only damage the State Department and the Foreign Service."*

His comments *"infuriated"* radical leftist Associate Justice Felix Frankfurter!

Straight, for many years a high level *"mole"* in the United States, explained: *"He summoned me to his chambers in the Supreme*

Court building and gave me a tongue lashing for my lack of courage.

'We must never be afraid to be identified with our friends!' he cried."

According to Straight *"friends"* is a Red mole's code word for other Communist moles secretly planted throughout the government hierarchy.

Is Michael Straight implying that Justice Frankfurter considered himself to be a Communist?

Yes!

And does Straight feel Frankfurter considered Acheson to be a communist as well?

Yes!

Offers Medford Evans: *"It would require more than ordinary skepticism to doubt that Frankfurter considered himself, Acheson, and Straight to be Communists."*

"Traitors to the United States have no cause to fear a legal penalty as they go about mobilizing to take over the nation in a violent, bloody revolution," charged the President Emeritus of

Harding College Dr. George S. Benson in 1970. *"Read that statement again.*

"It's true!

"The traitors know it's true.

"In Washington one of the top legal minds of the nation, who is also one of the best informed men in America on the ramifications of the Communist conspiracy, told us that the United States Justice Department could not arrest traitors or halt acts of treason now prevalent throughout the country.

"Supreme Court decisions of recent years so shattered the security laws that there's no workable safeguard against the mobilization, arming and training of a massive revolutionary force which is determined to seize control."

 Owen Lattimore (CFR) was Roosevelt's Special Advisor to Chiang Kai-shek when he headed the Nationalist Chinese government.

According to former Communist and *Daily Worker* editor Louis Budenz Professor Lattimore was a Communist!

Budenz testified that Lattimore had been carefully selected by Soviet intelligence *"to change the thinking here in Washington and in America on the Communist activities in China and its relations to the Soviet Union."*

In fact, former Soviet General Alexander Barmine named this spy as a member of Soviet Military Intelligence!

Lattimore stayed on with Truman after Roosevelt died.

Senator Joseph R. McCarthy first brought this security risk's Communist record to light in 1950.

Abe Fortas a fellow subversive was Lattimore's attorney!

Fortas would later be rewarded with an appointment to the Supreme Court by Lyndon Johnson!

Lattimore was again exposed by Senator William Jenner's Subcommittee: *"Owen Lattimore was, from sometime in the*

1930s a conscious, articulate instrument of the Soviet conspiracy."

Lattimore was finally indicted by a Federal Grand Jury on seven counts of perjury!

Each count was for lying about his Communist activities!

Abe Fortas

Incredibly at the bidding of Fortas the Justice Department quietly dropped all charges in 1955!

Despite his notorious Communist background Owen Lattimore was kept on at Johns Hopkins.

He was later welcomed back into the government in 1961 by President John F. Kennedy!

President Eisenhower according to former Red Party member Maurice Malkin in 1972 was suffering from the virus of appeasing the Communists.

He appointed as a payoff for election favors Earl Warren as Chief Justice of the Supreme Court.

Then followed the stoppage of prosecutions of Communists under the *Smith Act*.

Warren Court decisions had a major impact on America's internal security protection.

Important internal security laws were systematically voided.

No longer could Communist operatives dedicated to the destruction of the United States Government be made to name their associates under oath!

The right of a congressional committee to investigate Communism and Communists was severely restricted!

The Communist Party was no longer required to register as a subversive organization!

All these things came about despite the fact that the Supreme Court under Earl Warren reaffirmed in the mid-1960s that *"the Constitution of the United States is not a 'suicide pact.'*

"The Nation has the right and duty to protect itself from acts of espionage and sabotage, and attempts to overthrow the government by force."

Nevertheless the Supreme Court deliberately placed many obstacles in the path of investigating and exposing Communism and Communists in the United States.

M. Stanton Evans

M. Stanton Evans declared in 1965 that the court had *"laid level internal security statutes and regulations in almost every sector of American life.*

"The Court has erased from the books almost every sanction the United States has

against the internal activities of the Communists."

Martin Dies was for seven years chairman of the House Committee on Un-American Activities.

He had this to say in April of 1967: "*One by one the Court has destroyed every legal weapon which Congress and the states have constructed to defeat the treasonous activities of the domestic agents of the International Communist Conspiracy.*"

"*Where Congress and the states have legislated, the Court has invalidated,*" charged Dies. "*Where the FBI and the states' attorney Generals and our Bar Associations have moved to prevent sedition, the Court has remonstrated; where the Secretary of State and our Governors and loyal federal administrators have acted to remove Communists and subversives from vital positions in our government, the Court has reinstated.*"

"*The one area where there seems to be some predictability with respect to the Warren Court's action is where cases involved the interests of the world Communist conspiracy and its arm in this country, the Communist Party, USA,*" suggested Senator James O.

Eastland on May 2, 1962. *"It is moving*  *decision by decision, toward establishment of the Communist conspiracy in the United States as a legal political entity, with just as much right to exist and operate as any political party composed of decent patriotic American citizens.*

"When suppression would help the Communist cause, the Court suppressed.

"When preemption would help the Communist cause, the Court has pre-empted.

"When invention would help the Communist cause, the Court has invented.

"When misstatement would help the Communist cause, the Court has misstated."

"It would be extremely interesting to  *hear Mr. Justice Black try to explain how it was possible to believe that the Communists were right in every one of the hundred and two cases in which he participated,"* offered Revilo P. Oliver in December of 1963. *"Some members of it [the Supreme Court] have knowingly served the purposes of*

the Communist conspiracy, thus adding to the crime of judicial corruption the even greater crime of treason."

Journalist Susan Huck talked to Department of Justice attorneys years before the Internal Security Division was eliminated.

She was informed that they hadn't tried any cases involving Communist subversion for almost a decade!

No one wanted to bother prosecuting Reds or the Communist Party because they knew beforehand that the Supreme Court would ultimately throw the case out!

It's evident that the Internal Security Division of the Justice Department was effectively emasculated by pro-Communist Supreme Court decisions long before it was actually abolished!

Senate hearings were held in 1958 to create legislation to limit the Supreme Court's jurisdiction.

SPX Research Associates, a highly respected group of intelligence experts, concluded that *"decisions of the Supreme Court follow reestablished Communist lines."*

They further determined that *"the United States Supreme Court is the most powerful instrument of the Communist global conquest by paralysis. "*

The Supreme Court handed down a multitude of disastrous decisions favoring the Communist Party and individual Communists.

The nation's protective laws against subversives were either thrown out or rendered ineffective by the Court.

No longer does America have adequate safeguards!

Little can be done about those traitors who are systematically working towards the destruction of the Republic and the installation of a clone of Communist Occupied Russia in its place.

Here are but a few of the many cases which clearly illustrate how far the Supreme Courthas gone to aid and abet Communists and Communist activities in the United States.

In a 1941 hearing, Judge Charles Sears ruled that Harry Bridges was a Communist.

Bridges was President of the ILWU.

Or the International Longshoremen's & Warehousemen's Union!

Bridges was identified under oath as a communist agent by at least 35 witnesses including his first wife!

Sears further found that the Communist Party did advocate the violent overthrow of the United States Government!

Roosevelt nominated Francis Biddle to the position of Attorney General of the United States in 1941.

Biddle served in this position throughout most of World War II.

At President Truman's request he resigned after Roosevelt's death.

Truman shortly thereafter appointed Biddle as a judge at the Nuremberg Trials.

While Roosevelt's Attorney General he issued an order for the deportation of Bridges who was an Australian alien.

Then came a letter from the White House signed *"Eleanor."*

It ordered that the deportation of Bridges be held up!

Meanwhile the case was appealed.

Incredibly the Supreme Court said Bridges hadn't received a fair hearing regarding his Communist Party membership!

Even more astounding, Justice Frank Murphy declared there wasn't *"the slightest evidence introduced to show that either Bridges or the Communist Party seriously threatens to uproot the government by force and violence."*

He then had the unmitigated gall to declare that *"the Bridges case would stand forever as a monument to man's intolerance to man."*

The Immigration and Naturalization Service had most members of the Communist Party ready for deportation in 1956.

More than 10,000 alien Communists were going to be shipped back to their country of origin.

In another obvious act of Communist appeasement, the Supreme Court stepped in and crippled America's immigration system!

This was done deliberately to allow more Communists (and immigrants the Reds could control) to pour into the United States.

At the same time, extremely dangerous alien Communists such as Australian Harry Bridges, were allowed to stay in the country!

Maurice Malkin explained in 1972: *"Next came the liquidation of the anti-subversive sections of I & N and the dropping of all deportation cases against Moscow agents in the United States.*

"They were given a chance to regroup and reorganize into new fronts and penetrate civil rights and peace organizations."

Incredible?

Yes!

But true nonetheless!

The federal government was unwilling and often now unable to prosecute Communists.

Many states took it upon themselves to enact their own sedition laws that barred treasonous Communist activities within their borders!

The Supreme Court moved post-haste to disarm the states in this regard!

Communist Party leader Steve Nelson had been convicted in 1952 and sentenced to 20 years under Pennsylvania law.

The Supreme Court overturned Nelson's conviction on April 3, 1956!

This was no more than a ploy to free Communist criminals who had been convicted and imprisoned under sedition laws around the nation.

The decision voided the sedition laws in 42 states.

 On April 9, 1956, the Warren Court overturned the New York Supreme Court in favor of a Brooklyn College teacher named Harry Slochower!

He'd been fired for pleading the Fifth Amendment when questioned regarding his Communist Party membership and Red affiliations.

The Court deemed it unconstitutional for a school to dismiss a teacher who refused to discuss his Communist background.

Brooklyn College was forced to reinstate Slochower and pay $40,000 in back wages.

No longer could Reds be prohibited from teaching in tax-supported colleges and public schools.

It was ruled to be a denial of academic freedom to fire teachers who taught and advocated the use of force and violence to overthrow the government.

The *Summary Suspension Act* of 1950 allowed the firing of federal employees *"in the interest of the National Security of the United States."*

The Warren Court ruled on June 11, 1956, that it wasn't in the interest of national security to fire anyone for contributing services and money to Communist organizations!

The only exception might be if the federal employee was working in a *"sensitive position."*

The Court forced the federal government to rehire some *300* dangerous security risks!

Aliens have historically had a different status than citizens in the United States.

An alien can't vote and can't be drafted.

He or she is simply a foreign guest.

Yet the Supreme Court ruled on April 29, 1957, that the Attorney General can't even ask aliens if they've ever attended Communist Party meetings!

Rudolph Schware wasn't allowed to take the New Mexico Bar Examination.

The Board of Bar Examiners ruled that Schware's past membership in and loyalty to the Communist Party made him a man of *"questionable"* character.

The Supreme Court on May 6, 1957, ordered the Board to let Schware take the examination despite his subversive background.

"Lawyers are officers of the courts, and as such become an important and necessary part of our judicial system, declared former Congressman Dies in January of 1957. *"It would appear unthinkable that we should admit Communists to become officers in our judicial system,*

"When, therefore, the highest tribunal in our land denies to a Bar Committee the right to ask an applicant whether he is a Communist, it deprives us of a safeguard against the infiltration of our judicial system by the enemies of our country."

New Mexico union leader Clinton Jencks filed an affidavit in April of 1950, swearing he wasn't a Communist.

He was prosecuted by the Justice Department and convicted for perjury.

The Warren Court overturned the conviction on June 3, 1957.

Why?

Because Jencks wasn't allowed to see the FBI data used as evidence against him!

This perverse ruling required that all reports by witnesses now be given to the disloyal individuals in cases involving Reds.

The Communist defendant must be told precisely how the evidence was obtained.

The Court ordered disclosures would reveal to the Communist leadership exactly who the informants were.

Subversive revolutionaries were no longer prosecuted!

Why?

Because the information disclosed could cause more harm than would allowing the Communist to go free.

Justice Tom C. Clark dissented: *"Unless the Congress changes the*

51

rule announced by the Court today, those intelligence agencies of our government, engaged in law enforcement, may as well close up shop, for the Court has opened their files to the criminal and has afforded him a Roman holiday for rummaging through confidential information, as well as vital national secrets."

As a result of the Jencks case, the Court of Appeals later ruled that the Communist Party was not required to register as a subversive organization per the order of the Subversive Activities Control Board.

Why?

Because the FBI hadn't shown the Party their secret reports on its subversive activities!

"In 1948, for the first time since the 1920's, the Party found itself on the defensive when the Department of Justice initiated prosecution against its leaders," explained FBI Director J. Edgar Hoover in 1958. *"The twelve members of the Party's National Board were indicted under the Smith Act.*

"In a long trial, running through most of 1949, eleven members were convicted.

"In June, 1951, the Supreme Court upheld these convictions.

"The government subsequently took prosecutive action against additional Party leaders.

"This government prosecution was a strong disabling blow against the Party.

"Many of its top leaders were arrested and convicted.

"Others lived in fear of arrest. As a result, the Party to a large extent went underground. "

Attorney Roy Cohn described the trial in 1968: *"The display of bad manners and improper conduct by lawyers and witnesses for the defense was the worst this country has ever seen.*

"The Communists did not fear conviction.

"Following instructions, they sought to turn the courtroom into a forum for their cause.

"The Party had instructed them that they were expendable and they accepted it.

"In the courtroom they laughed at us, at our judicial methods, at our judges."

The *Alien Registration Act (Smith Act)* case handled by the Warren Court was a disaster for American internal security.

The 1940 *Act* simply prohibited any conspiracy that advocates the overthrow of the United States Government by force and violence.

It was also unlawful for anyone to belong to a group advocating this.

Lastly, the *Smith Act* required the finger printing of all aliens in the United States.

Jack Hall was a well known Communist Party organizer.

He worked undercover in the Communist dominated ILWU in Hawaii on orders from Moscow.

The Senate Internal Security Subcommittee disclosed on November 21, 1956: *"By 1955, Communist political and economic control of Hawaii through Communist dominated unions was so great that the official Communist Party went out of existence.*

"Since 1955, Communist propaganda and other activities have been conducted through the unions."

In 1953, Jack Hall was charged with conspiring to overthrow the U.S. Government by force.

Hall was convicted of violating the *Smith Act.*

But his conviction, as well as many others, was overturned in 1957 by the Warren Court!

On June 17, 1957, the Supreme Court reversed two lower court rulings regarding the *Smith Act.*

It was no longer a crime for a Communist to advocate and teach the violent overthrow of the government.

Such activity was not illegal, even if there was *"evil intent"* said the Court so long as this was *"divorced from any effort to instigate action to that end."*

New trials were ordered for nine convicted Communist Party leaders.

Five others were acquitted!

J. Edgar Hoover revealed that every one of the 49 top Party leaders who'd been imprisoned for advocating the overthrow of the government were freed by the Supreme Court.

Further prosecution of Communists under the *Smith Act* was stopped!

A top Communist Party functionary described the ruling as the greatest legal victory the Party had ever received!

Congressional investigations were further emasculated by the Supreme Court under the leadership of Chief Justice Earl Warren on June 17, 1957.

The Court questioned whether or not congress had the right to investigate and publicize cases of Communist subversion.

The Court ruled that this *"involved a broad scale intrusion into the lives and affairs of private citizens."*

The conviction of John Watkins for contempt of congress was overturned.

The Court held that a witness was not required to reveal the names of associates, even though he'd admitted to being involved in Communist activities.

The Supreme Court ruled on June 17, 1957, that a sovereign state had no right to ask a state employee questions regarding subversive activities.

New Hampshire's Attorney General, said the Court, didn't have the authority to question Professor Paul Sweezy of New Hampshire University.

Sweezy had refused to answer, when asked *"Do you believe in Communism?"*

And *"Did you advocate Marxism at that time?"*

The Court agreed that he had the right to do so.

John Stewart Service was caught in the act of giving classified documents to Soviet espionage agents in 1945.

He was finally fired six years later in 1951 under provisions of the *McCarran Act.*

This *Act* gave the Secretary of State the responsibility of dismissing an employee in the interest of national security.

Several lower courts refused to set aside this traitor's dismissal.

End of story?

Not hardly!

The Supreme Court on June 17, 1957, ordered Service reinstated with back pay!

This dangerous security risk's guilt was never challenged!

Improper procedures were said to have been used in his firing.

Service, obviously with the assistance of Comrades in high places, was ultimately assigned a diplomatic plum.

He became American Consul in Liverpool, England.

Security risk Arthur Goldberg (CFR) became Kennedy's Secretary of Labor.

He'd worked closely with Robert Wirtz, Communist Party organizer and Secretary of the Illinois Communist Party.

Goldberg was past president of the Chicago chapter of the National Lawyers Guild.

In this capacity, he worked under the direction of David J. Bentall and Isaac E. Ferguson -- two important Reds who were involved in founding the Communist Party in the United States.

The NLG was cited as *"the foremost legal bulwark of the Communist Party, its front organizations, and controlled unions."*

Goldberg, despite his consistently subversive background *(more probably because of it)* was chosen to replace suspected Communist Felix Frankfurter on the Supreme Court.

One of LBJ's leftist friends, advisors and Supreme Court appointees was security risk Abe Fortas!

His notorious record of association with Communists, affiliation with Communist fronts and questionable financial dealings forced him to resign from the Supreme Court in 1969.

Chicago Tribune columnist Walter Trohan offered this: *"His best friends were members of one or another of the Communist cells which were fermenting under the care of Henry Wallace."*

Fortas was a close friend of Communist spies Alger Hiss, Lee Pressman, John Abt, Harry Dexter White and many others!

He was subversive Owen Lattimore's attorney when Lattimore was exposed by Senator Joe McCarthy in 1950.

Lattimore was correctly branded two years later by Senator William Jenner's Internal Security Subcommittee as *"a conscious articulate instrument of the Soviet conspiracy."*

Fortas also assisted Lattimore in writing *Ordeal by Slander.* This was no more than a thinly veiled attempt to smear and discredit the gutsy anti-Communist McCarthy.

Lyndon Johnson had a penchant for nominating subversives to the Supreme Court!

Thurgood Marshall was his second atrocious selection.

Astoundingly, the Senate hastily confirmed this Harvard leftist in 1967.

Why?

The media said nothing!

Why?

Marshall was a member of the International Judicial Association (IJA).

So was Abe Fortas and his two Soviet spy friends from the Roosevelt days Nathan Witt and Lee Pressman.

The IJA was described thusly: *"From its inception, the International Juridicial Association has specialized in the defense of individual Communists or of the Communist Party itself."*

Many identified Communists were members of the IJA.

Included were:

61

Joseph R. Brodsky
Leo Gallagher
David J. Bentall
Isaac E. Ferguson

Cora Weiss King

Marshall and Fortas were both on the Executive Board of the National Lawyers Guild.

The SISS reported: *"To defend the cases of Communist lawbreakers, fronts have been devised.*

"Among these organizations is The National Lawyers Guild."

Marshall was one of the top ACLU officials in the Soviet controlled International Labor Defense, organized specifically to be the legal arm of the international Red conspiracy.

Congressman Martin Dies noted: *"When the House Committee on Un-American Activities wrote in 1944 that 'there is not a single important Communist-front organization which does not have a substantial representation from the personnel of the International Juridicial Association, it surely did not contemplate that by 1966 the Supreme Court of the United States would be added to the list."*

Notoriously pro-Communist Earl Warren was appointed by President Eisenhower to be Chief Justice of the United States Supreme Court.

Earl Warren was a man who spent some of his vacations with Communist Occupied Yugoslavia's murderous dictator Tito.

Warren blatantly lied when he charged the *"right wing" (anti-Communist movement)* with the November 22, 1963, assassination of President John F. Kennedy!

Warren spent other of his vacations in the Crimea.

There he spent much of his spare time visiting with Nikita Khrushchev the Neanderthal *"Butcher of Budapest."*

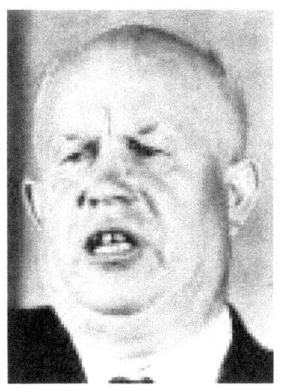

Warren, following the communist propaganda line lied again when he claimed the assassination of President Kennedy was *"a result of the hatred and bitterness that has been injected into the life of our nation by bigots."*

Communist Occupied Russia's *Tass* all the while knew the assassin was one of their own!

Yet this official Party organ called it the work of *"racists, the Ku Klux Klan and the Birchists."*

The Soviet *New Times* followed suit and said it was *"an act of ultra-Right political terror."*

The *Daily Worker* demanded that Warren be appointed to head an investigation of the despicable murder!

Lyndon Johnson dutifully obeyed the demand of the *Daily Worker*!

Warren was given the job!

The *New York Daily News* editorialized: *"In view of the Earl Warren Supreme Court's long-standing tenderness toward Communists, any report this commission may give birth to will be open to suspicion of pro-Communist bias."*

The Warren Commission's sole task appears to have been to hide the Soviet Union's involvement in the assassination of an American President!

They succeeded!

Glossed over or ignored were a number of extremely important facts about ACLU member Lee Harvey Oswald.

According to David Emerson Gumaer, Oswald *"joined the ACLU shortly before his major role in the assassination of the President of the United States.*

"Although the Warren Report mentions Oswald's ACLU membership someone has deliberately omitted all reference to the ACLU from the Warren Report index."

FBI Director J. Edgar Hoover called Oswald a *"dedicated Communist."*

His physically abused Russian wife, Marina, was the ward of a KGB Colonel.

Oswald had previously tried to assassinate General Edwin A. Walker but the bullet missed by inches!

He wrote: *"In the event of war I would kill any American who put a uniform on in defense of the American government -- any American."*

An avid Marxist as a teenager, Oswald refused to salute the flag in school.

While a marine, he was jokingly referred to as *"Comrade Oswaldkowich."*

Lee Harvey Oswald was unquestionably an assassin in the employ of Communist Occupied Russia!

He had been meticulously trained in the Soviet Union in guerrilla warfare!

In sabotage!

In terrorism!

And as an assassin!

The biased Warren Commission did its job well!

It successfully prevented evidence of a Moscow directed conspiracy in Kennedy's assassination from reaching the American people!

The deceptive report is believable only by people who still wait for Santa Claus on Christmas Eve and look for the Bunny to come on Easter morning!

It is widely accepted in intelligence circles to be no more than a whitewash for a major KGB operation!

Former Congressman Martin Dies rings forth a point to ponder: *"At no time has the President or any official speaking for our government, except J. Edgar Hoover, said frankly that President Kennedy was murdered by a Communist whose record was well-known to our intelligence agencies, but who was permitted to roam at large even when the President's car passed within a rifle shot of the place he worked."*

Another major victory for the Communist Party in the United States was realized on November 15, 1965.

The Warren Court struck down the *Internal Security Act of 1950!*

The Court ruled it was unconstitutional *(on the basis of self-incrimination)* to force Communists to register with the Attorney General.

In an eight-to-nothing decision, the Court said that "*registration as a Communist party member and information asked on the registry form might be used as evidence in, or at least supplementary leads to, a criminal prosecution under the Smith Act of 1940 or other criminal statutes.*"

This ruling allowed the Red revolutionaries to proceed unhampered in their goal of ultimately overthrowing the government.

The Communists no longer had to be concerned about being picked up and jailed during a national emergency.

Gus Hall General Secretary of the Communist Party USA was overjoyed.

This fanatic said the decision would stimulate the *"growth of the Communist Party now.*

"It will be possible to be more openly active in all fields."

 Hall's bloodthirsty nature was shown when he said at the 1961 funeral of Eugene Debs: *"I dream of the hour when the last congressman is strangled to death on the guts of the last preacher -- and since the Christians love to sing about the blood, why not give them a little of it?"*

Communist Archie Brown gained national notoriety in 1959 while leading the San Francisco riots against the House Committee on Un-American Activities.

 This Red was the underling of the notorious Communist union leader Harry Bridges.

Brown had been convicted and sentenced to six months in prison for serving on the Executive Board of Local 10 of the Red controlled ILWU.

It was a crime at that time for a Communist to be a labor union official.

In 1965 the Warren Court ruled that such a law was unconstitutional!

Alexander Haig had all the makings of a true American hero.

Where on the road to fame and success was he captured by the political left?

He graduated from the U.S. Military Academy at West Point in 1947.

He served in Europe, Asia and Vietnam.

He worked in the Nixon White House for identified Soviet spy Henry *"Bor"* Kissinger.

Haig served as White House Chief of Staff under President Nixon during the Watergate scandal in 1974.

He later served as NATO commander from 1974-79.

Alexander Haig (CFR) was the top assistant and highly polished protégé of identified Kremlin spy Henry Kissinger.

Interestingly, Haig said: *"Over a period, Henry and I developed a special rapport.*

"From my perspective, I found most of his views compatible with mine."

Not only was Alexander Haig the protégé of Comrade Kissinger but of two other notorious subversives as well -- Robert S. McNamara (CFR) and Cyrus Vance (CFR).

These security risks had been heavily involved in running the treasonous no-win Vietnam War!

Alexander Haig played a most important role in the humiliating cut and run surrender of all Vietnam to the North Vietnamese Communists.

Haig was also the shadowy power behind the creation of the disastrous Legal Services Corporation.

This was one of the most corrupt of all government agencies.

It was nothing more than a scurrilous department developed solely for providing federal subsidies for swarms of radical far left lawyers.

Despite his subversive background Haig was selected to be Reagan's Secretary of State!

Predictably and understandably Haig made absolutely no effort to clean security risks out of the State Department!

This all important question still begs an answer!

Where on his road to fame and success and power did Alexander Haig capitulate to the political left?

Epilogue

The record covering crucial episodes of the McCarthy era has been massively and deliberately distorted from the very beginning!

Conveniently forgotten or deliberately overlooked are the 78 hearings held between 1951 and 1952 by Senator William E. Jenner's (R-Indiana) Senate Internal Security Subcommittee (SISS); the House Committee On Internal Security; the House Un-American Activities Committee (HUAC) under the chairmanship of both Martin Dies (D-Texas) and Francis Walters (D-Pa); the Federal Bureau of Investigation (FBI) under the guidance of J. Edgar Hoover; and other investigating committees and individuals.

Out of all of these investigations one man was selected:

To be stopped!

To be destroyed!

To be made an example!

Why?

So that no one would ever again dare to initiate any investigations into the penetration of our government agencies by communist agents (spies) in the employ of the Soviet Union!

Yes!

An obscure Senator from Wisconsin was deliberately targeted for this purpose!

Joseph McCarthy's incredibly successful investigations panicked those on the political left.

Their reaction was shockingly quick!

Key data was been suppressed, denied and even widely falsified.

This took place in the media, all branches of government and many alleged scholars entrenched in the ivory towers of our institutions of higher learning!

Such misreporting and misrepresentation of the facts continues today.

Much of the misinformation we were (and still are today) so carefully spoon-fed about Senator Joseph McCarthy the man and his investigations was no more than an admixture of uncheckable blovations from deceased third parties and demonstratable falsehoods!

For example, how many innocent people were harmed by McCarthy's revelations?

The correct answer?

Not one!

No!

Not One!

McCarthy's most virulent critics have had more than a half century to produce the names of the hundreds of innocent people they claim were destroyed by the astounding revelations of the Senator from Wisconsin.

Yet those highly skilled propagandists in our media and government and institutions of higher learning have been unable to name even one innocent person they claim was destroyed after being falsely accused by McCarthy!

How many innocent people committed suicide as a result of McCarthy's exposure?

The correct answer?

Not one!

Not one suicide can be attributed to the investigations conducted by McCarthy!

No! Not one!

According to the obscene claims made the highly skilled propagandists in our media, government and scholars entranced in those ivory towers of our colleges and universities there were a rash of suicides with bodies falling constantly of the heads of pedestrians below on the streets of Manhattan!

Once again, McCarthy's most virulent critics have had more than 50 years to produce the names of the hundreds of innocent people they claim committed suicide because of the astounding revelations of the Senator from Wisconsin.

Yet those highly skilled propagandists in our media and government and institutions of higher learning have been unable to name even one innocent person they claim committed suicide after being falsely accused by McCarthy!

No!

Not one!

But there were two suicides on record during the McCarthy period!

Neither was the result of an innocent person who'd been ruined by McCarthy's revelations!

Both were subversives who'd been exposed by McCarthy!

Both were subversives who'd been positively indentified as Kremlin agents!

Lawrence Duggan had been operating in the State Department as a widely known Soviet spy!

He'd been called to testify before a Congressional investigating committee.

Duggan never made it!

He conveniently "fell" from a window high up in a Manhattan skyscraper!

Fell?

Probably not!

He was more than likely pushed from or tossed out of the window by an assassin in the employ of the Soviet Union!

Why?

To make certain he didn't fold under pressure and start naming other Kremlin moles.

Secondly there was the unexpected demise of Harry Dexter White.

This Soviet agent discovered that he was being investigated by J. Edgar Hoover of the FBI!

He died of a sudden heart attack!

Coincidence?

Not hardly!

Was White's death a suicide?

Yes or at least so claimed McCarthy's critics!

Again, not hardly!

Heart attacks can readily be induced with the proper use of certain medicines administered by a hired assassin in the employ of the Kremlin!

Why?

Simply to eliminate anyone who might panic and decide to turncoat and reveal the names of other spies secretly entrenched deeply in the bowels of every branch of our government.

To sum up, most fit into one of three categories:

Conscience lacking incurable liars!

Those with an axe to grind!

Individuals who simply do not know the facts!

If you liked this book in the *None Dare Call It Treason* series then you'll probably also enjoy reading the others!

Gift copies of this book can be ordered at

robertwpelton.com or amazon.com

Available Titles

None Dare Call It Treason Book 1
The Internal Security Farce!
5.5" x 8.5" 97 pages $4.95
Order from robertwpelton.com
or amazon.com

None Dare Call It Treason Book 2
Never Ending Subversion In Government!
5.5" x 8.5" 202 pages $4.95
Order from robertwpelton.com
or amazon.com

None Dare Call It Treason Book 3
America's Subversive State Department
Bloated With Security Risks
5.5" x 8.5" 202 pages $4.95
Order from robertwpelton.com
or amazon.com

None Dare Call It Treason Book 4
America's Illustrious State Department!
It's Machiavellian Misdeeds!
5.5" x 8.5" 202 pages $4.95
Order from robertwpelton.com
or amazon.com

None Dare Call It Treason Book 5
Our Presidents A Major Security Threat!
5.5" x 8.5" 202 pages $4.95
Order from robertwpelton.com
or amazon.com

None Dare Call It Treason Book 6
Presidential Words & Deeds &Blatant Lies!
5.5" x 8.5" 202 pages $4.95
Order from robertwpelton.com
or amazon.com

None Dare Call It Treason Book 7
Subversives Close To Our Presidents
5.5" x 8.5" 89 pages $4.95
Order from robertwpelton.com
or amazon.com

None Dare Call It Treason Book 8
Henry Kissinger
The Shadowy Untouchable Kremlin Spy!
5.5" x 8.5" 202 pages $4.95
Order from robertwpelton.com
or amazon.com

None Dare Call It Treason Book 9
Inexcusably Arming America's Enemies!
5.5" x 8.5" 202 pages $4.95
Order from robertwpelton.com
or amazon.com

None Dare Call It Treason Book 10
Inexcusably Financing America's Enemies!
5.5" x 8.5" 202 pages $4.95
Order from robertwpelton.com
or amazon.com

None Dare Call It Treason Book 11
*Treasonous   Trade With & Aid To
Enemies Of Freedom!*
5.5" x 8.5" 202 pages $4.95
Order from robertwpelton.com
or amazon.com

None Dare Call It Treason Book 12
Wholesale Treason During the War In Vietnam!
5.5" x 8.5" 202 pages $4.95
Order from robertwpelton.com
or amazon.com

None Dare Call It Treason Book 13
Big Business & Astounding Acts Of Treason!
5.5" x 8.5" 202 pages $4.95
Order from robertwpelton.com
or amazon.com

None Dare Call It Treason Book 14
Illegally Importing Slave Made Goodies!
5.5" x 8.5" 202 pages $4.95
Order from robertwpelton.com
or amazon.com

None Dare Call It Treason Book 15
The House That Hiss Built
The Anti-American United Nations!
5.5" x 8.5" 202 pages $4.95
Order from robertwpelton.com
or amazon.com

None Dare Call It Treason Book 16
Security Risks in the House and Senate!
5.5" x 8.5" 202 pages $4.95
Order from robertwpelton.com
or amazon.com

None Dare Call It Treason Book 17
*The Supreme Court A Devastating
Threat To National Security!*
5.5" x 8.5" 202 pages $4.95
Order from robertwpelton.com
or amazon.com

Orders for Resale
40% Off Retail Price

Send Purchase Order to

christianamerica2@yahoo.com

MEET THE

AUTHOR

Robert W. Pelton has been writing and lecturing for more than 45 years on political, religious and historical subjects.

He has published more than 100 books including the exposé *Unwanted Dead or Alive. The betrayal of American POWs Following World War II, Korea and Vietnam.*

Robert W. Pelton proudly claims a heritage going all the way back to well before the War for American Independence.

One of Pelton's ancestors John Rogers came to America on the Mayflower and was one of 41 signers of the *Mayflower Compact.*

John Smith was one of the founders of Jamestown.

Peleg Pelton served as a fifer in the Continental Army at age 17 during the Battle of Saratoga (1777) and at Yorktown (1781).

Captain Peter Hager was Commander of the Old Stone Fort in Schoharie, New York, in 1780.

Another, Captain Bezaleel Tyler fought in the only Revolutionary War Battle taking place in Sullivan County, New York.

Mr. Pelton is a member of Sons of the Revolution (SOR), and Sons of the American Revolution (SAR).